SCHOLASTIC

MAPS FOR THE OVERHEAD

NEIGHBORHOODS & COMMUNITIES

10 Color Transparencies, Mini-Lessons, and Activities That Teach Essential Map Skills

by Catherine M. Tamblyn

NEW YORK • TORONTO • LONDON • AUCKLAND • SYDNEY
MEXICO CITY • NEW DELHI • HONG KONG • BUENOS AIRES

Teaching *Resources*

Dedication

To AJK

Cover design by Josué Castilleja
Cover illustration by Mike Moran
Interior design by Holly Grundon
Interior illustrations by James Graham Hale

Book ISBN 0-439-56819-6
Product ISBN 0-439-54049-6
Copyright © 2004 by Catherine M. Tamblyn
Maps copyright © 2004 by Scholastic Inc.
All rights reserved.
Printed in the U.S.A.

6 7 8 9 10   40   11 10 09 08

Contents

Teaching With Map Transparencies

Map Work Activity Pages

How to Use This Book

Maps for the Overhead:
Neighborhoods & Communities
*is designed to encourage active map
learning and investigation of places
most familiar to primary children.
This useful guide offers a variety
of map skill activities based on 10
colorful transparencies contained
in the front pocket. Each map
transparency can be used to teach,
model, and review a different map skill.
Plus, they all have themes uniquely related
to neighborhoods and communities.*

Each map transparency is supported by a teaching guide section at the beginning
of the book and at least one related reproducible activity at the back of the book.
The teaching guide section for each transparency is divided into four parts:

1. **Getting Started:** Links the map skill with the real world and
   students' prior knowledge, and creates motivation for students
   to learn the skill.

2. **Teaching With the Transparency:** Offers strategies for using
   the map transparency with the overhead projector in a whole-
   class setting. This section includes ideas for modeling the map
   skills as well as large-group instruction activities for helping
   students understand how to read the different maps and
   understand information presented in map form.

3. **Questions to Explore:** Suggests critical thinking questions
   that help further students' understanding of the concepts
   presented in each map.

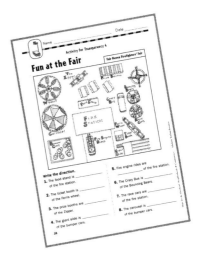

4. **To Do:** Provides links to the student reproducibles at the back of the book. Reproducibles marked with the overhead projector icon require students to view the transparency in order to complete the activity. Reproducibles marked with the pencil icon can be completed independent of the transparency, either in the classroom or as a homework assignment. You may wish to copy some of the reproducibles onto clear transparencies to model how students might work through the answers.

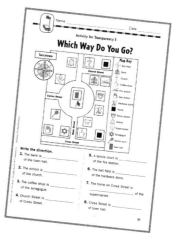

The reproducible section of this book also includes fun, manipulative cutouts for use with the map projection. These cutouts personalize the projection and extend its use. They may be affixed to the projection with painter's tape.

Transparencies are a fun and engaging way to teach basic map skills to young children as well as enhance their exploration of the world. They are excellent for whole-group instruction. By allowing children to write on the map transparency or interact with the map projection, children feel special and remain on task. Children's active participation also allows you to check their understanding of the map skill as they locate places and things or explain their thinking to classmates. With this book and the map transparencies inside, children will develop practical map skills that they can link to their everyday lives and find out that maps can be so much FUN!

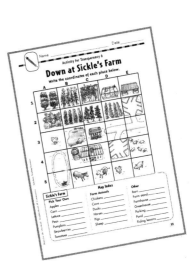

My Backyard

Skill:
Reading a backyard map using a map key with picture symbols

Getting Started

Discuss with children: Say you're having a party. What might be a good way to show your friends how to get to your home? When someone mentions a map, ask children what kinds of things they might see on a map.

Teaching With the Transparency

Display Transparency 1 on the overhead projector. Explain to children that the picture shows a *map*, or a flat drawing of a place. Point out that the view of this map is from directly above. Point to and explain the use of these map parts:

- **title** – name of the map; it tells what the map shows and is sometimes in a box

- **map region** – main part of the map

- **map key** – box with a list of symbols on the map

- **picture symbols** – small pictures that stand for real things

- **symbol names** – next to symbols; they tell what symbols mean

Tell children that there are two ways they can read a map:

1. They can choose a symbol in the map key, read its name, then find that symbol on the map.

2. They can choose a symbol on the map, find it in the key, then say the name for it.

Invite children to carefully study the projection to see if all map symbols are in the key. Guide children to notice that a symbol for lawn is not included. Ask how this symbol might look, and have a volunteer draw it and write its name in the key on the transparency.

Challenge children to name a symbol that appears more than once on the map. (*Tree*) Ask children: Why aren't there three tree symbols in the map key?

To Do

- Photocopy and distribute "What's in My Backyard?" (page 16) to each student. Have children answer the questions, either individually or in small groups.

Questions to Explore

- What is a map?

- What does a map's title tell?

- What is the difference between a map and a map key?

- What are symbols?

- Why are symbols used on maps?

- Why do we use maps?

- Where would you need to be to see land from the view of this map?

Pirate's Cove Playground

Skill:
Using direction words to determine location on a playground map

Getting Started

Ask children: What words do you use to explain where something is? Help children generate words that name location, such as *near*, *far from*, *next to*, *behind*, *between*, *to the left*, *to the right*, *middle*, and *on*. Write a list on the board.

Teaching With the Transparency

Display Transparency 2 on the overhead and invite volunteers to come up and point to the different parts of the map, such as the title, map key, symbols, and symbol names. Ask: What do you think this map shows? (A *playground*) How can you tell? Invite children to read the symbol names in the map key and locate those symbols on the map.

Invite students to use the words on the board to tell the location of things or playground equipment on this map. For example, the fort is *between* the slides on the super slide, or the tire swings are *next to* the pirate's ship.

Rotate the map transparency to give children more opportunities to use direction words. Point out that the words *between*, *middle*, and *on* remain constant regardless of the map's position.

To Do

◆ Personalize the projection by adding Kid Cutouts. Photocopy page 31 so that each child has his or her own kid cutout. Distribute the cutouts and invite children to decorate and write their names on them. Then invite them to affix their cutouts on the map projection with painter's tape. Have children take turns using direction words to describe the location of their cutouts on the projected map. Encourage children to draw additional playground items on the projection and describe their location.

◆ Photocopy and distribute "Playground Fun" (page 17) to each student. Have children answer the questions, either individually or in small groups.

Questions to Explore

◆ How can direction words help us find things?

◆ What would happen if you did not use these words?

◆ When do you mostly use direction words?

◆ What other direction words name location? (*Under, beside, top, below, behind*)

Tiny Town

Skill:
Reading a community street map with abstract symbols

Getting Started

Display Transparency 3 on the overhead, covering the symbol names on the map key. Invite children to read the map's title and to tell what the map shows. Challenge children to guess what the symbols mean. Students may find it difficult to decipher the shapes, lines, patterns, and colors. Explain that these types of symbols are called *abstract symbols*. Ask: How are these different from other map symbols you've seen so far? (*The other map symbols look similar to the things they represent; abstract symbols use simple shapes, lines, colors, and so on to represent different places.*) Uncover the symbol names so students can read what they mean.

Teaching With the Transparency

Randomly point to places on the map transparency and have children use the key to tell what the places are. Ask children: What's another way to tell where these places are besides pointing to them? Guide children to notice the street addresses on the map. Help them read street names, tracing the streets from one point to another and discussing how they intersect. Identify street corners. Invite volunteers to come up and draw Xs on the map projection where traffic lights might appear. Name places in Tiny Town and have children identify the street(s) that they are on and places that are across the street from each other.

Add Kid Cutouts (page 31) to the projection. Have children write their names on the cutouts and use painter's tape to affix them on one of the homes. Encourage children to take turns naming the streets on which their cutouts "live" and identifying their next-door neighbors.

To Do
◆ Photocopy and distribute "Around Town" (page 18) to each student. Have children answer the questions, either individually or in small groups.

◆ Invite children to create a street map of their neighborhood similar to the one on Transparency 3. Photocopy and distribute "My Neighborhood" (page 19) to each student.

Questions to Explore

◆ How are abstract symbols different from picture symbols?

◆ How are maps of towns helpful?

◆ Who might use a map of a town?

◆ What places would be on a map of your neighborhood? Of your town?

Fair Haven Firefighters' Fair

Skill:
Using a compass rose with cardinal directions to determine location on a fairground map

Getting Started

Display Transparency 4 on the overhead. Ask children to read the map's title and tell what the map shows. Call on volunteers to read the labels on the map to identify the attractions and places on the fairground. To reinforce the concept that maps are drawings of real places, relate this map to neighborhood and community fairs children might have attended.

Teaching With the Transparency

Point out the compass rose on the upper right-hand corner of the map and ask children if they know what it is. Explain that the compass rose is a tool that tells direction on a map. Explain that the letters stand for the four main directions on Earth: *north*, *south*, *east*, and *west*. You may wish to write the word for each cardinal direction next to its letter abbreviation. Tell children that these directions are called *cardinal directions*.

Demonstrate how to use the compass rose to find cardinal directions. Ask a volunteer to find the Wipeout on the map. Ask a second volunteer to find the Carousel. Pointing to both attractions, explain to children that the Wipeout is *north* of the Carousel. Repeat with other pairs of attractions.

To Do

◆ Encourage children to draw additional attractions on the projected map, such as a balloon vendor or a pony ride. Ask them to use cardinal directions to describe their location.

◆ Photocopy and distribute "Fun at the Fair" (page 20) to each student. Have children answer the questions, either individually or in small groups.

Questions to Explore

◆ How could cardinal directions have helped with setting up this fairground?

◆ Could cardinal directions help you tell a friend where rides are?

◆ What other direction words could you use to have someone find you?

◆ Where else besides a map do you read cardinal directions?

Terrytown

Skill:
Using a compass rose with intermediate directions to determine location on a community map

Getting Started

Display Transparency 5 on the overhead. Ask children to read the map's title and tell what the map shows. Have them read symbol names in the key and locate the places on the map, both by pointing to them and by saying the street names that the places are on.

Teaching With the Transparency

Direct children's attention to the compass rose on the map and introduce intermediate directions. Explain that NE stands for *northeast*. Ask children: What do you think NW, SE, and SW stand for? (*Northwest, southeast, and southwest*) Point out that intermediate directions are between the cardinal directions. Explain that we use intermediate directions when two places are not exactly north, south, east, or west of each other. Write the words for intermediate and cardinal directions next to the letter abbreviations.

Invite two volunteers to locate the gas station and the police station on the map. Ask: Where is the gas station in relation to the police station? (*Southwest*) Repeat with other places.

To Do

◆ Draw arrows on the transparency to show how and in which direction traffic might flow around the circle on Main Street. Then give children a copy of the Car Cutout (page 31). Encourage children to use the car on the projection to show a route from one place to another, and use the compass rose to describe the direction they're going.

◆ Photocopy and distribute "Which Way Do You Go?" (page 21) to each student. Have children answer the questions, either individually or in small groups.

Questions to Explore

◆ How can intermediate directions better name the location of a place than cardinal directions?

◆ Where else besides a map might you read intermediate directions?

◆ What kinds of workers might use intermediate directions?

Sickle's Farm

Skill:
Using a grid map and map index to locate things on a map of a farm

Getting Started

Display Transparency 6 on the overhead. Ask children to read the map's title and tell what the map shows. Invite children to compare this map with other maps they have seen earlier. If necessary, switch back and forth between Transparency 5 (Terrytown) and Transparency 6 (Sickle's Farm) to give children a frame of reference. Point to the grid lines, letters, and numbers as children call them out.

Teaching With the Transparency

Explain to children that this type of map is called a *grid map*. Point out that lines go across and down to form squares. Explain that the squares put together show a whole map. The squares by themselves show tiny parts of the map. Point to individual squares and have children tell what they see.

Demonstrate how to read a grid map. Explain that all squares across the first row are 1s and that all squares down the first column are As. To name a square, you give the number and letter of a square. For example, the topmost, left-hand square is 1-A. Point to other squares and ask children to name them.

Direct children's attention to the map index below the grid map. Explain that the map index is a tool that helps us find things on a grid map. It lists all places and things on the map and names the squares where they are found. Use the map index to locate places and things on the map.

To Do

◆ Photocopy and distribute "Name That Square" (page 22) to each student. Have children answer the questions, either individually or in small groups.

◆ Give each child a copy of "Down at Sickle's Farm" (page 23). Have children fill in the map index by writing the coordinates of places on the map.

◆ Encourage children to create their own grid maps using the Blank Grid Map (page 24). Assign partners and have children exchange maps to complete each other's map indexes.

Questions to Explore

◆ How would a grid map be helpful for visitors to Sickle's Farm?

◆ Where would you go on this farm and which parking lot would be closest to it?

◆ If row F was added to the map, what would square 3-F show?

Minton Mini Mall

Skill:
Reading a floor plan map of a shopping mall

Getting Started

Ask children if they've ever been to a shopping mall. Explain that a mall is a large building with many stores. Ask: What might help shoppers find different stores in a mall? (A *map*)

Teaching With the Transparency

Display Transparency 7 on the overhead. Explain to children that the map on the screen is called a *floor plan*. A floor plan usually shows rooms in a home or a building. It can also show the arrangement of furniture in a room. Explain that this map features the floor plan of a mall, showing the different stores. Point out that this floor plan also has a map index and a map key. Invite children to read the symbol names in the map key and locate those symbols on the map.

Model two ways to read the map and map key, and use these methods to locate places:

1. Choose a number on the floor plan. Find the same number in the map index. Read the name of the room or store next to that number.

2. Choose a room or store in the map index. Find the room or store with the same number on the floor plan.

To Do
◆ Photocopy and distribute "Gone Shopping" (page 25) to each student. Have children answer the questions, either individually or in small groups.

◆ Give each child a copy of "My School Floor Plan" (page 26). Challenge children to draw a floor plan of your classroom or school to help visitors find their way around.

Questions to Explore

◆ How can floor plans like this one help shoppers?

◆ Where might you find a floor plan in a store or mall?

◆ Where have you seen or used a floor plan?

Mountain Lakes

Skill:
Reading a physical land-use map with abstract and picture symbols

Getting Started

Display Transparency 8 on the overhead. Ask children to read the map's title and tell what the map shows. Have children read the symbol names for landforms and bodies of water in the key and locate these color or abstract symbols on the map. Invite volunteers to draw on personal knowledge to describe each landform and body of water. Explain to children that this kind of map is called a *physical map*.

Teaching With the Transparency

Have children read the names for picture symbols on the key and locate them on the map. Point out that these symbols show how people can use the land and water in Mountain Lakes. Call out the letter for each campground and have children locate each one. Ask them to name the kind of land on which each campground is located and trace the road used to reach each one.

Ask children to describe the difference between the horse and hiking trails. Have them trace each trail and name the type of land or body of water each one crosses or encircles.

To Do

◆ Discuss other ways people could use the land and water on this map. Invite children to affix the Map Symbol Cutouts (page 27) on the map projection to show other land use. Encourage them to draw their own symbol on the blank cutout. Ideas may include: dirt biking, motorboating, sailing, rock climbing, or snowboarding. Be sure to add the map symbol cutouts to the map key and write labels for each.

◆ Photocopy and distribute "Back to Nature" (page 28) to each student. Have children answer the questions, either individually or in small groups.

Questions to Explore

◆ How could this map help visitors to Mountain Lakes?

◆ Which campground would you use? Why?

◆ What kinds of land and water would you show on a map of your community?

◆ What symbols would you use to show how people in your community use land and water?

Arbor County

Skill:
Reading a political map and determining
distances between towns

Getting Started

Display Transparency 9 on the overhead. Call on volunteers to point to
and name parts of the map, such as the title, map key, and compass rose.
Ask children: What do you think this map shows? Direct children to the
map key to guide their guesses.

Teaching With the Transparency

Explain to children that this kind of map is called a *political map*.
Political maps show communities and often use a dot as the symbol for
communities. Ask children: What kind of community is shown by the
dot symbol on this map? (*Town*) Invite children to count the number of
towns on the map. Explain to children that a *county* is one of the parts
into which a state or country is divided. Have children name the three
counties shown on the map and trace their borders. Ask children: Which
county does the map feature? (*Arbor County*)

Direct children's attention to the numbers on the map. Tell them that
the numbers show how many miles there are between towns in Arbor
County. Ask a volunteer to come up and locate Forest Hills on the map.
Then have another volunteer find Pine Bluffs. Ask children: How many
miles are between Forest Hills and Pine Bluffs? (9) Continue to name
pairs of towns connected by one road and have children tell the miles
between them. For extra challenge, name pairs of towns connected by
two or more roads and have children add the miles to find the total
distance between towns. Have children use the compass rose to tell the
direction from one town to another. For example, Redwood Falls is
southeast of Aspen.

To Do

◆ Photocopy and distribute "County Life" (page 29) to each student.
Have children answer the questions, either individually or in small
groups.

Questions to Explore

◆ Why are miles on maps helpful?

◆ What can you learn about Arbor County from this map?

◆ If your town was part of Arbor County, how would it be shown on this map?

Jeeter Park

Skill:
Identifying routes and locating places
on a city park map

Getting Started

Display Transparency 10 on the overhead. Ask children: What do you
think this map shows? (A park) Direct children's attention to the map
key and ask them to find the symbol for path. Review directions by
inviting volunteers to come up and trace the paths on the south, east,
and north sides of the park. Then ask volunteers to describe the
directions of the straight paths inside the park, using the fountain
as a point of reference.

Teaching With the Transparency

Explain to children that a *route* is a way one travels from one place to
another. Choose two places on the map, such as the bike rental and the
picnic area. Invite a volunteer to come up and trace a route between
places. Invite another child to come up and trace a different route. Ask
children: If someone is in a hurry, which route do you think that person
should take? Discuss the fastest or shortest and the slowest or longest
routes. Encourage children to describe routes using cardinal or
intermediate directions and road names if applicable. Discuss starting
and ending points of routes.

Let children take turns affixing Kid and Car Cutouts (page 31) on the
projection. They can pretend they are meeting a friend at a cutout's
location and give oral directions to that spot.

To Do

◆ Photocopy and distribute "A Day at the Park" (page 30) to each
student. Have children answer the questions, either individually or
in small groups.

Questions to Explore

◆ What is a route?

◆ What routes
do you take
every day?

◆ Where does
your route start?
Where does it
end?

◆ How do you use
routes at home?
at school?
in your
community?

◆ Why might you
need to know
the fastest route
to a place?

◆ Why might you
want to take the
longest route to
a place?

◆ Why is it helpful
to know two
different routes
to the same
place?

Name _____ Date _____

Activity for Transparency 1

What's in My Backyard?

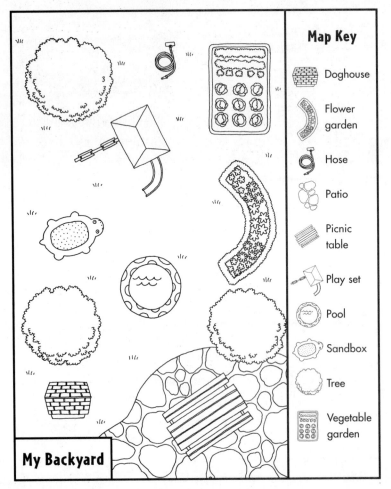

My Backyard

Map Key
- Doghouse
- Flower garden
- Hose
- Patio
- Picnic table
- Play set
- Pool
- Sandbox
- Tree
- Vegetable garden

1. What is the map's title?

_____

2. How many symbols are in the map key?

_____

3. What is the turtle symbol?

_____

4. What home is on the map?

_____

5. How many trees are on the map?

_____

6. What gardens are on the map?

_____

7. What is the picnic table on?

_____

8. What symbol is on the map but not in the key?

_____

16

Maps for the Overhead: Neighborhoods & Communities Scholastic Teaching Resources

Activity for Transparency 2

Playground Fun

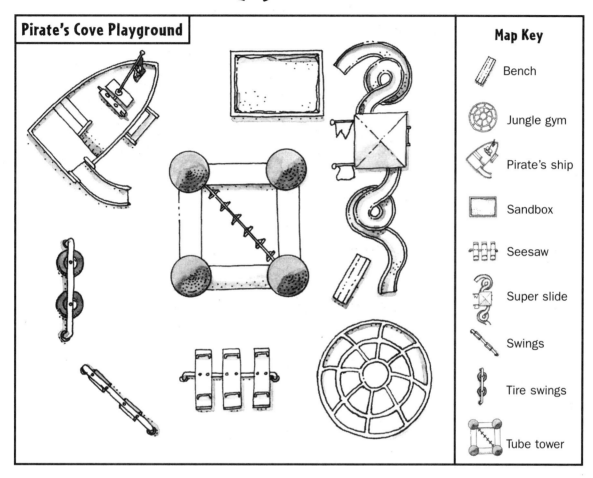

Pirate's Cove Playground

Map Key

Bench

Jungle gym

Pirate's ship

Sandbox

Seesaw

Super slide

Swings

Tire swings

Tube tower

Write the thing.

1. The _____ is in the middle of the playground.

2. The jungle gym is to the right of the _____.

3. The _____ is to the left of the sandbox.

4. The _____ are between the pirate's ship and the swings.

Write the direction word.

5. Two flags are on the _____ side of the super slide.

6. The seesaw is _____ the swings and the jungle gym.

7. A flag is _____ the pirate's ship.

8. The bench is to the _____ of the tube tower.

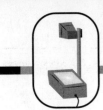

Activity for Transparency 3

Around Town

Tiny Town

Little Lane

Teeny Avenue

Bitsy Boulevard

Small Street

Map Key

☆ Community center

▷ Fire station

□ Home

◯ Library

✿ Park

◇ Police station

⬡ Post office

♻ Recycling center

▨ Restaurant

⌐ School

□ Store

✚ Street

◯ Town hall

1. On which street is the school?

_____

2. Which street has no stores?

_____

3. Which street has the most stores?

_____

4. How many homes are on Little Lane? _____

5. What is next to the fire station?

_____

6. What is next to the police station?

_____

7. On which street is the library?

_____

8. What is to the left of the community center? _____

Maps for the Overhead: Neighborhoods & Communities   Scholastic Teaching Resources

Activity for Transparency 3

My Neighborhood

Draw a street map of your neighborhood.
Make a key to show your home and other places.

My Neighborhood		Map Key

Activity for Transparency 4

Fun at the Fair

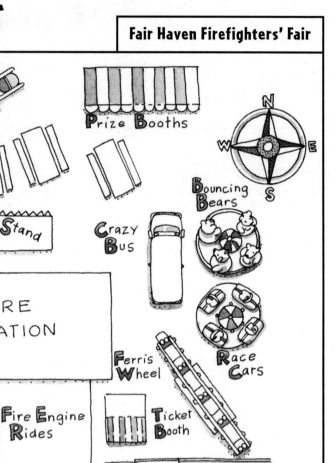

Fair Haven Firefighters' Fair

Write the direction.

1. The food stand is _____ of the fire station.

2. The ticket booth is _____ of the Ferris wheel.

3. The prize booths are _____ of the Zipper.

4. The giant slide is _____ of the bumper cars.

5. Fire engine rides are _____ of the fire station.

6. The Crazy Bus is _____ of the Bouncing Bears.

7. The race cars are _____ of the fire station.

8. The carousel is _____ of the bumper cars.

Name _____ Date _____

Which Way Do You Go?

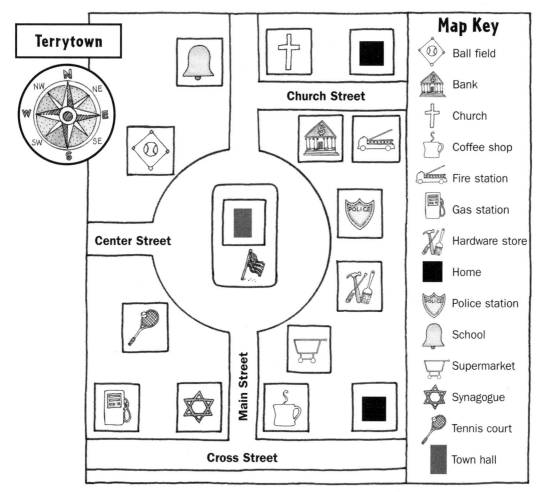

Map Key

- ◇ Ball field
- 🏛 Bank
- ✝ Church
- ☕ Coffee shop
- 🚒 Fire station
- ⛽ Gas station
- 🔨 Hardware store
- ■ Home
- 🛡 Police station
- 🔔 School
- 🛒 Supermarket
- ✡ Synagogue
- 🎾 Tennis court
- ▮ Town hall

Write the direction.

1. The bank is _____ of the town hall.

2. The school is _____ of the church.

3. The coffee shop is _____ of the synagogue.

4. Church Street is _____ of Cross Street.

5. A tennis court is _____ of the fire station.

6. The ball field is _____ of the hardware store.

7. The home on Cross Street is _____ of the supermarket.

8. Cross Street is _____ of town hall.

Activity for Transparency 6

Name That Square

Write the coordinates.

1. Where can corn be picked? _____

2. Where are the pigs? _____

3. Where are the chickens? _____

4. Where is the barn? _____

5. Where can cars park? _____

6. Where is the farmer's home? _____

7. Where does the driveway start? _____

8. Where can people buy fruits and vegetables? _____

Maps for the Overhead: Neighborhoods & Communities   Scholastic Teaching Resources

Activity for Transparency 6

Down at Sickle's Farm

Write the coordinates of each place below.

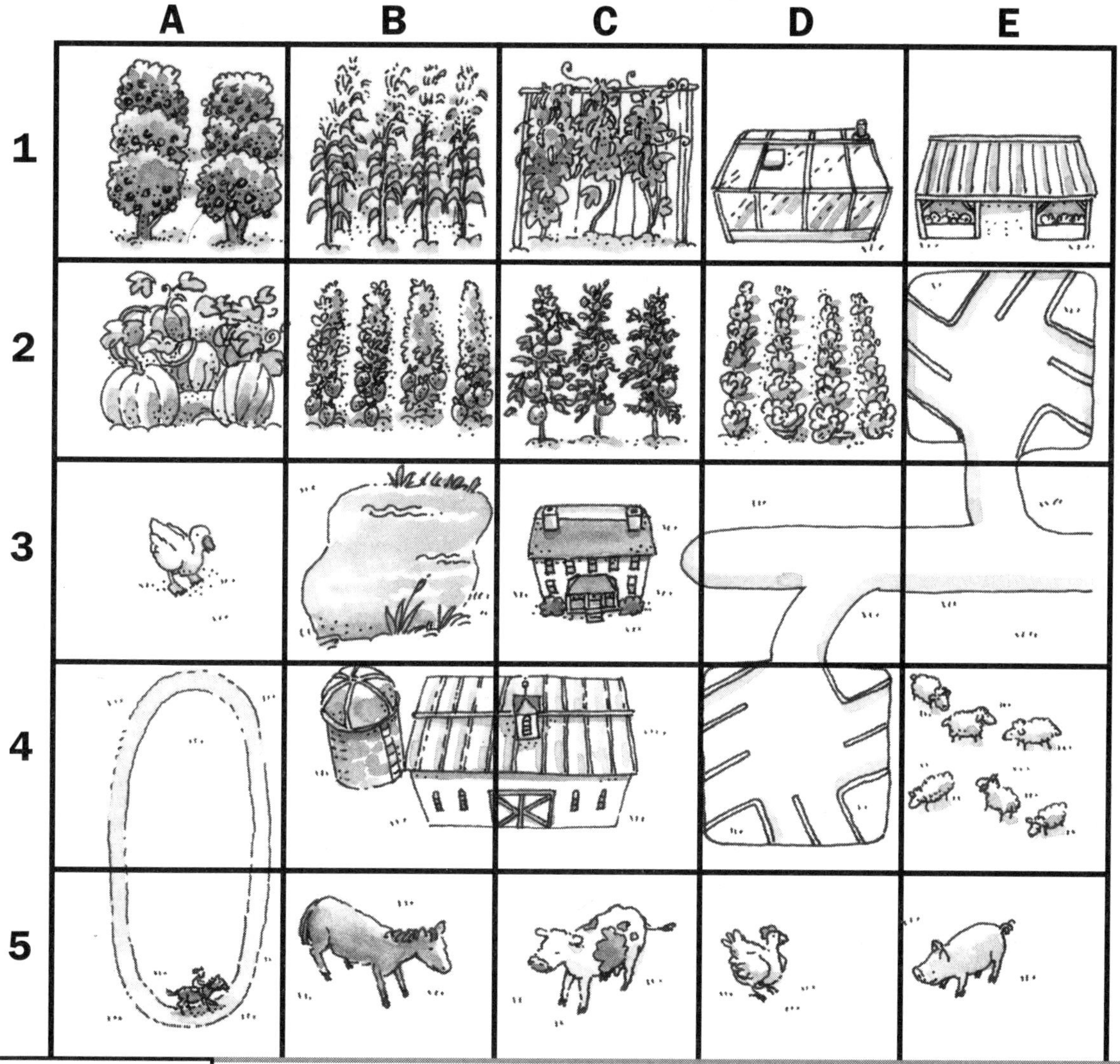

	A	B	C	D	E
1					
2					
3					
4					
5					

Sickle's Farm

Map Index

Pick Your Own

Apples _____

Corn _____

Lettuce _____

Peas _____

Pumpkins _____

Strawberries _____

Tomatoes _____

Farm Animals

Chickens _____

Cows _____

Ducks _____

Horses _____

Pigs _____

Sheep _____

Other

Barn _____

Farm stand _____

Farmhouse _____

Greenhouse _____

Parking _____

Pond _____

Riding lessons _____

Activity for Transparency 6

Blank Grid Map

Make your own grid map. Write each place in the map index below. Then write the coordinates.

	A	B	C	D
1				
2				
3				
4				

Map Title: _____

Map Index

_____	_____	_____
_____	_____	_____
_____	_____	_____
_____	_____	_____

Maps for the Overhead: Neighborhoods & Communities   Scholastic Teaching Resources

Activity for Transparency 7

Gone Shopping

Minton Mini Mall

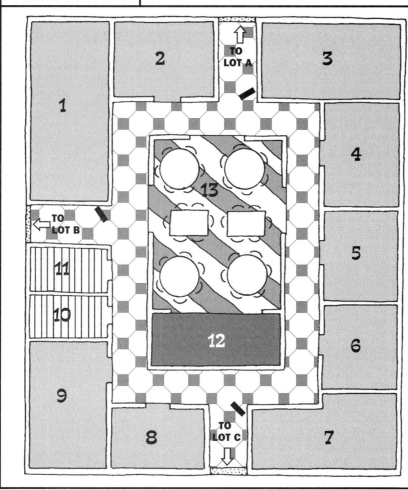

Map Index

The Candy Jar **6**
Clothes Corner **7**
Courtyard **13**
Courtyard Cafe **12**
Dot's Dollar Store **5**
Gifts and Gadgets **3**
Gold Tinker **8**
Hot Shot Photography **4**
Men's Restroom **11**
Sid's Shoes **2**
Sport Spot **1**
Toy Masters **9**
Women's Restroom **10**

Map Key

— Door
Entrance
Fast Food
Hall
Mall Map
Rest Area/Tables
Restroom
Store

1. What is store 6? _____

2. In what store could you buy a toy? _____

3. Where could you shop for shoes? _____

4. What store is next to Gifts and Gadgets? _____

5. Which store is next to the entrance for Parking Lot B? _____

6. How many mall maps are there? _____

7. Where can you sit in the mall? _____

8. Where do you walk to go from store to store? _____

Name _____   Date _____

Activity for Transparency 7

My School Floor Plan

Draw a floor plan of your school. Give each place its own number. Then list the places and their numbers in the map index.

Map Index

Maps for the Overhead: Neighborhoods & Communities   Scholastic Teaching Resources

Activity for Transparency 8

Map Symbol Cutouts

Draw your own symbol in the blank box.

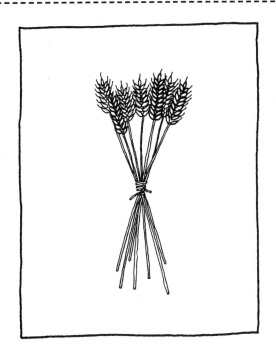

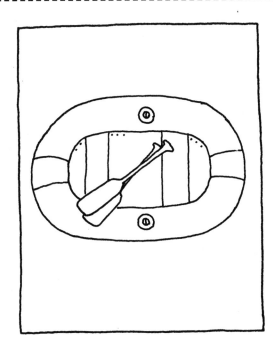

Activity for Transparency 8

Back to Nature

1. Which lake has swimming and fishing?

   _____

2. How many campgrounds are there?

   _____

3. In what direction is campground A from B?

   _____

4. From what landform does Rapid River flow?

   _____

5. Around which lake is the hiking trail?

   _____

6. What can people do on Rapid River?

   _____

7. Which trail crosses the river?

   _____

8. What is south of the hills?

   _____

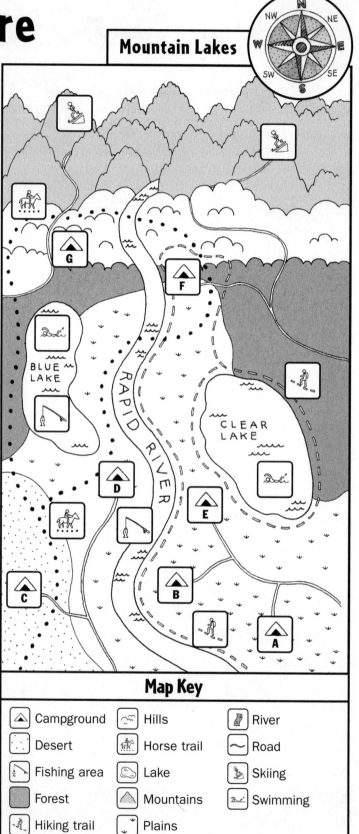

Mountain Lakes

Map Key

▲ Campground	Hills	River
Desert	Horse trail	~ Road
Fishing area	Lake	Skiing
Forest	Mountains	Swimming
Hiking trail	Plains	

Maps for the Overhead: Neighborhoods & Communities   Scholastic Teaching Resources

Activity for Transparency 9

County Life

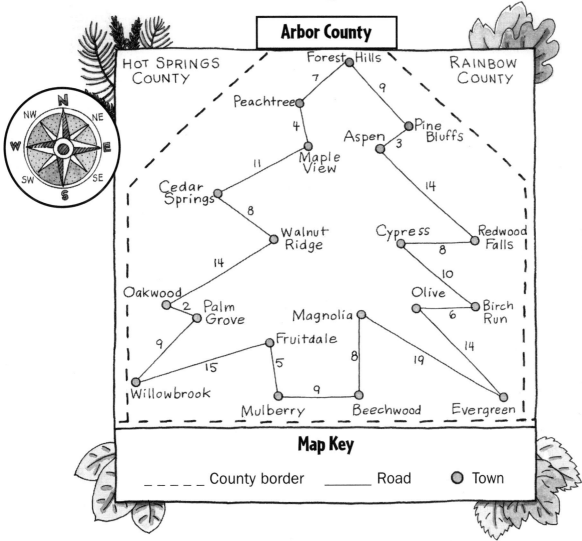

Write the direction.

1. Evergreen is _____ of Olive.

2. Cypress is _____ of Birch Run.

3. Beechwood is _____ of Magnolia.

4. Forest Hills is _____ of Peachtree.

Write how many miles.

5. Cedar Springs to Walnut Ridge

_____

6. Oakwood to Willowbrook _____

7. Cypress to Olive _____

8. Fruitdale to Beechwood _____

Activity for Transparency 10

A Day at the Park

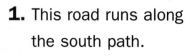

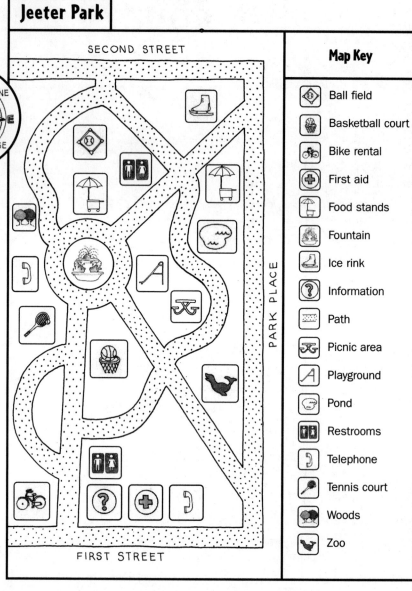

Jeeter Park

SECOND STREET

PARK PLACE

FIRST STREET

Map Key

- Ball field
- Basketball court
- Bike rental
- First aid
- Food stands
- Fountain
- Ice rink
- Information
- Path
- Picnic area
- Playground
- Pond
- Restrooms
- Telephone
- Tennis court
- Woods
- Zoo

1. This road runs along the south path.

_____

2. This road runs along the east path.

_____

3. This road runs along the north path.

_____

4. The ice rink is along this path. (Write the direction.)

_____

5. The zoo is along this path. (Write the direction.)

_____

6. First aid is along this path. (Write the direction.)

_____

7. It is southwest of the fountain.

_____

8. It is east of the fountain.

_____

Maps for the Overhead: Neighborhoods & Communities   Scholastic Teaching Resources

For Transparencies 2, 3, 5, and 10

Kid and Car Cutouts

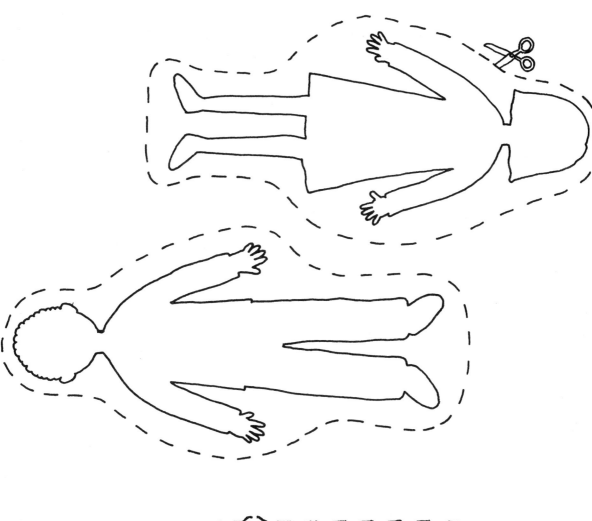

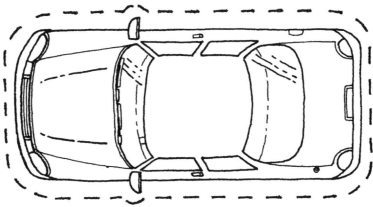

Selected Answer Key

What's in My Backyard? (p. 16)
1. My Backyard
2. 10
3. sandbox
4. doghouse
5. 3
6. flower, vegetable
7. patio
8. lawn or grass

Playground Fun (p. 17)
1. tube tower
2. seesaw
3. pirate's ship
4. tire swings
5. left
6. between
7. on
8. right

Around Town (p. 18)
1. Little Lane
2. Teeny Avenue
3. Small Street
4. 6
5. town hall
6. post office
7. Bitsy Boulevard
8. restaurant

Fun at the Fair (p. 20)
1. N or north
2. W or west
3. E or east
4. E or east
5. S or south
6. W or west
7. E or east
8. N or north

Which Way Do You Go? (p. 21)
1. NE or northeast
2. W or west
3. E or east
4. N or north
5. SW or southwest
6. NW or northwest
7. SE or southeast
8. S or south

Name That Square (p. 22)
1. 1-B
2. 5-E
3. 5-D
4. 4-B, 4-C
5. 2-E, 4-D
6. 3-C
7. 3-E
8. 1-E

Down at Sickle's Farm (p. 23)
Apples: 1-A
Corn: 1-B
Lettuce: 2-D
Peas: 1-C
Pumpkins: 2-A
Strawberries: 2-B
Tomatoes: 2-C
Chickens: 5-D
Cows: 5-C
Ducks: 3-A
Horses: 4-A, 5-A, 5-B
Pigs: 5-E
Sheep: 4-E
Barn: 4-B, 4-C
Farm stand: 1-E
Farmhouse: 3-C
Greenhouse: 1-D
Parking: 2-E, 4-D
Pond: 3-B
Riding lessons: 4-A, 5-A

Gone Shopping (p. 25)
1. The Candy Jar
2. Toy Masters or 9
3. Sid's Shoes or 2
4. Hot Shot Photography
5. Sport Spot or 1
6. 3
7. Courtyard or 13
8. Hall

Back to Nature (p. 28)
1. Blue Lake
2. 7
3. SE or southeast
4. mountains
5. Clear Lake
6. fish
7. horse trail
8. forest

County Life (p. 29)
1. SE or southeast
2. NW or northwest
3. S or south
4. NE or northeast
5. 8 miles
6. 11 miles
7. 16 miles
8. 14 miles

A Day at the Park (p. 30)
1. First Street
2. Park Place
3. Second Street
4. NE or northeast
5. SE or southeast
6. S or south
7. tennis court
8. playground